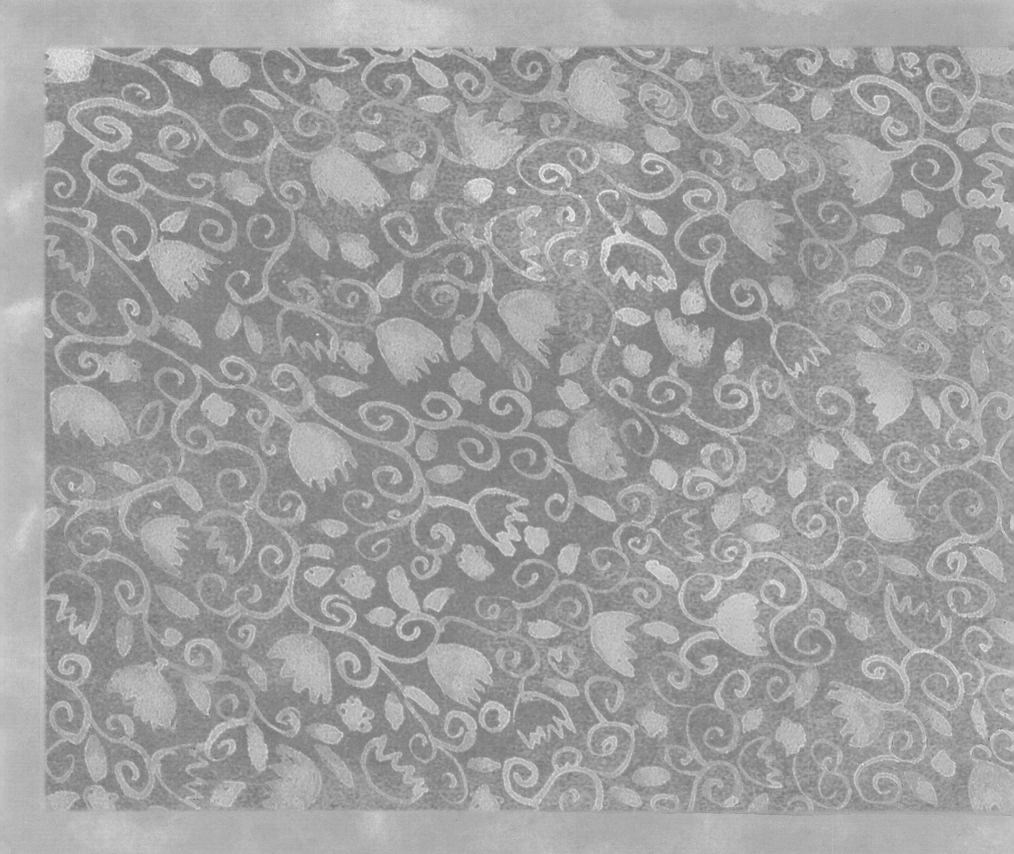

Voyage à travers l'art islamique

Journey through Islamic Art

Na'ima bint Robert & Diana Mayo

mantra

J'ai entendu des histoires sur les villes de Samarkand et de Bagdad,
sur les Moghols en Inde et les Maures en Espagne.

*I heard tales about the cities of Samarkand and Baghdad,
About the Moghuls in India and the Moors in Spain.*

J'ai amassé les fils de soie de l'histoire dans mes mains et,
avec eux mon esprit a tissé une cape volante :
une cape qui m'a entraînée dans un voyage extraordinaire
à travers l'art du monde islamique.

I gathered silken threads of history in my hands and,
With them, my mind wove a flying cloak:
A cloak that took me on an amazing voyage
Through the art of the Islamic world.

Ma cape m'a emmenée dans la vieille ville de Bagdad,
avec ses mosquées, ses bains publics,
ses champs de course et ses pavillons.

My cloak took me to the old city of Baghdad,
Home to mosques, public baths,
racetracks, and pavilions.

Avec ses châteaux fortifiés dans le désert,
ornés de peintures murales qui vont
du plafond jusqu'au sol.
Samarra abrite la plus grande mosquée du monde,
j'ai imaginé que l'appel à la prière parvenait
jusqu'à moi dans les nuages.

Home to fortified desert castles,
Adorned with wall-paintings from floor to ceiling.
The largest mosque in the world called Samarra its home,
I imagined that the call to prayer reached me in the clouds.

Ma cape m'a emmenée dans l'Espagne islamique,
où l'Est rencontre l'Ouest.
Je suis passée près des savants, des inventeurs
et des astronomes de la cour,
qui testaient les limites des connaissances humaines.

My cloak took me to Muslim Spain,
Where the East met the West.
I passed scientists, inventors and court astronomers,
Testing the limits of human knowledge.

Là, j'ai erré dans des cours décoratives,
près des fontaines et des jardins parfumés.

There, I wandered through ornamental courtyards,
Past fountains and scented gardens.

L'héritage artistique d'Islam
et d'Espagne ont fusionné
pour créer le palais de
l'Alhambra et la grande
mosquée de Cordoue.
Des dômes, des mosaïques et
des arches ont accueilli
mes yeux avides.

The artistic heritage of
Islam and Spain
Fused to create the
Al Hambra palace and
the great mosque of
Cordoba.
Domes, mosaics and
archways greeted my
eager eyes.

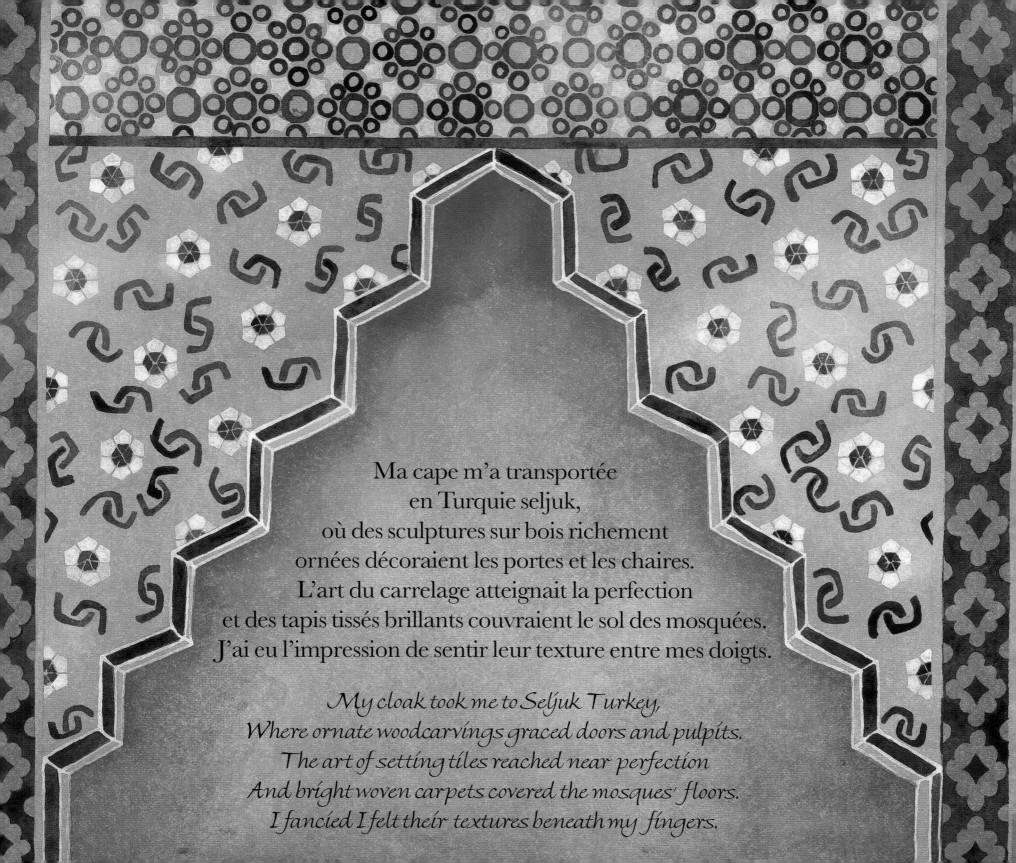

Ma cape m'a transportée
en Turquie seljuk,
où des sculptures sur bois richement
ornées décoraient les portes et les chaires.
L'art du carrelage atteignait la perfection
et des tapis tissés brillants couvraient le sol des mosquées.
J'ai eu l'impression de sentir leur texture entre mes doigts.

My cloak took me to Seljuk Turkey,
Where ornate woodcarvings graced doors and pulpits.
The art of setting tiles reached near perfection
And bright woven carpets covered the mosques' floors.
I fancied I felt their textures beneath my fingers.

Ma cape m'a emmenée
au Samarkand de Timur le boiteux
où les artisans du monde entier
étaient rassemblés.

*My cloak took me to the Samarkand
of Timur 'the Lame'
Where artisans from around the world
were gathered.*

Des tailleurs de pierre d'Inde,
des calligraphes de Perse,

*Stonemasons from India,
calligraphers from Persia,*

des orfèvres de Turquie et
des tisseurs de soie de Damas.

*Silversmiths from Turkey and
silk-weavers from Damascus.*

Tous ramenés captifs pour embellir sa ville,
alors que son palais était une tente, il fut nomade jusqu'au bout.

All brought back as captives, to beautify his city,
While his palace was a tent – a nomad to the end.

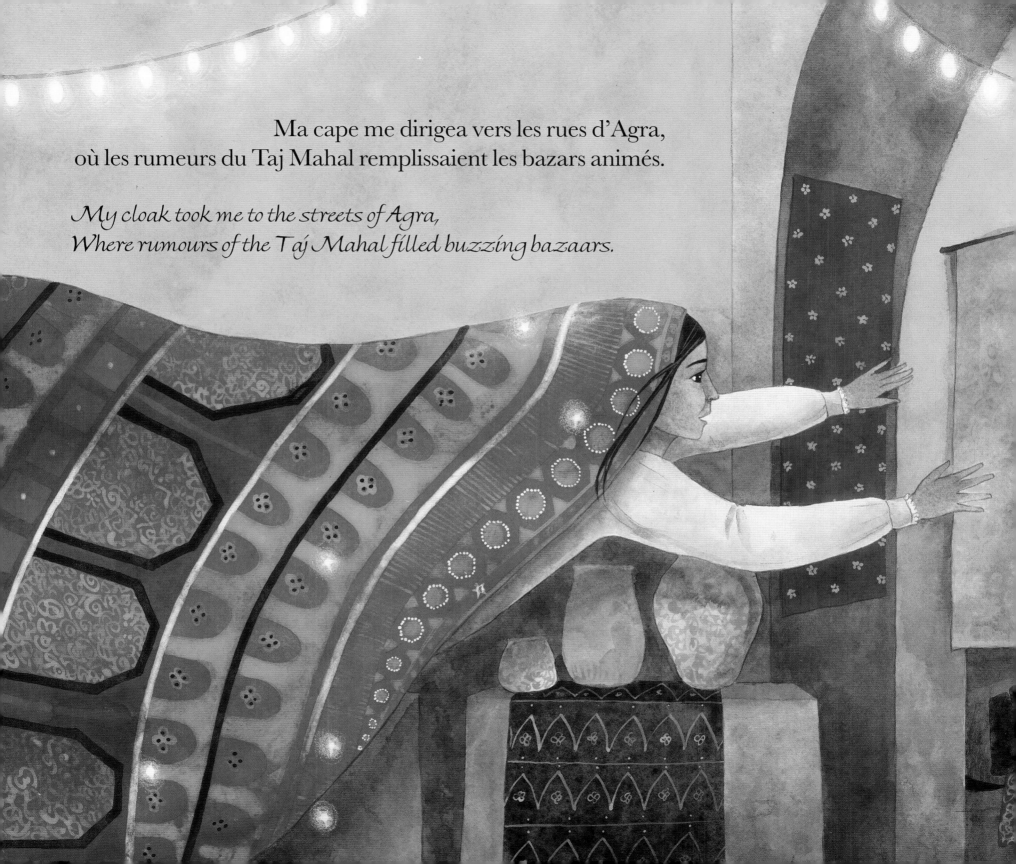

Ma cape me dirigea vers les rues d'Agra,
où les rumeurs du Taj Mahal remplissaient les bazars animés.

My cloak took me to the streets of Agra,
Where rumours of the Taj Mahal filled buzzing bazaars.

Un bâtiment né d'une promesse faite sur un lit de mort,
son revêtement de marbre
scintillait dans la lumière.

A building born from a deathbed promise,
Its garment of white marble
Shimmered in the light.

المشرق

Les inscriptions calligraphiques du Coran,
les arabesques à fleurs et les dessins géométriques
s'harmonisaient toutes et les poètes l'on appelé
« le visage brillant de l'aube. »
J'ai fait le souhait que sa beauté puisse honorer
les vivants plutôt que d'enchâsser les morts.

صباح الفجر

Calligraphic inscriptions from the Qur'aan,
Floral arabesques and geometric designs
all harmonised
And the poets named her 'Dawn's bright face'.
I wished its beauty could grace the living
and not enshroud the dead.

Ce voyage était un rêve, une fantaisie d'enfant,
bien que toutes ses destinations soient réelles.
J'espère que votre cape sera tissée par ce conte
et que vous aussi, vous irez là-bas.

This voyage was a dream - a child's fantasy,
Though all its destinations are true.
I hope that your cloak will be spun by this tale
And that you will go there too.

Here are some explanations to help you enjoy the story:

Samarra
In the 9th century, after the foundation of Baghdad, the Caliph (ruler) moved his capital to the splendid city of Samarra. The Great Mosque was once the largest mosque in the Islamic world and rises to a height of 52 meters.

Islamic Spain was established in the 8th century by Muslims from North Africa who were known as Moors. For over three hundred years, Muslims, Christians and Jews lived together in a Golden Age when learning, art and culture flourished.

Seljuk Turkey was one of the eras in Islamic history. The Seljuks were Muslim rulers who took control of Persia and Turkey. Seljuk Turkey became the centre of excellence in weaving, ceramic painting and wood carving.

Born in the 14th century, **Timur 'the Lame'**, also known as Tamerlane, was a fierce and determined Mongol warrior who loved art. Whenever his armies invaded foreign cities, he would take care to protect the artisans and take them back to beautify his city, Samarkand.

The **Taj Mahal** was a monument built by the Mughal Emperor Shah Jahan in 1631 as a tribute to his loving wife Mumtaz Mahal. Legend says that she made him promise to build her a mausoleum more beautiful than any the world had ever seen.

Arabesque is an art form originally from Asia Minor. It was later adapted by Muslim artisans into a highly formalised form of intertwined flowers and plants.

The Qur'aan, the Muslim holy book, was revealed to the Prophet Muhammad (pbuh) by the Angel Gabriel. Its verses are often inscribed in beautiful patterns by calligraphers.

First published in 2005 by Mantra Lingua
Global House, 303 Ballards Lane, London N12 8NP
www.mantralingua.com

Text copyright © 2005 Na'ima bint Robert   Illustrations copyright © 2005 Diana Mayo
French translation by Gwennola Orio-Glaunec
Dual language copyright © 2005 Mantra Lingua
All rights reserved

A CIP record for this book is available from the British Library.

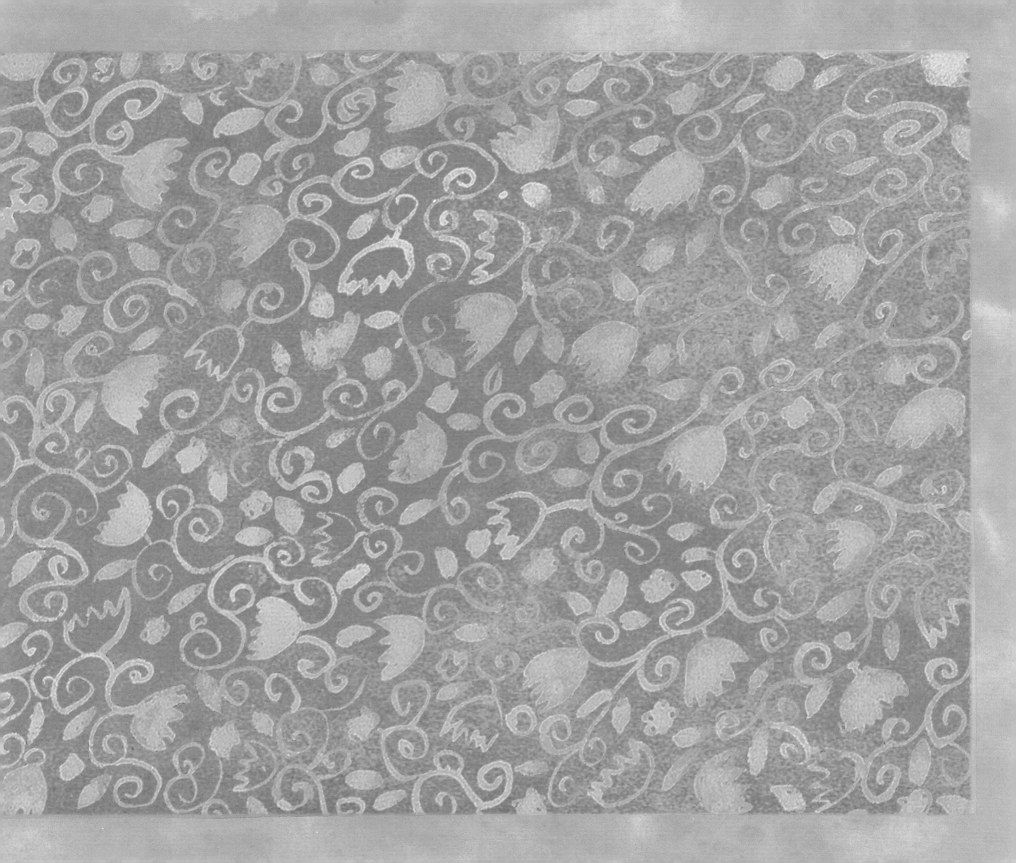

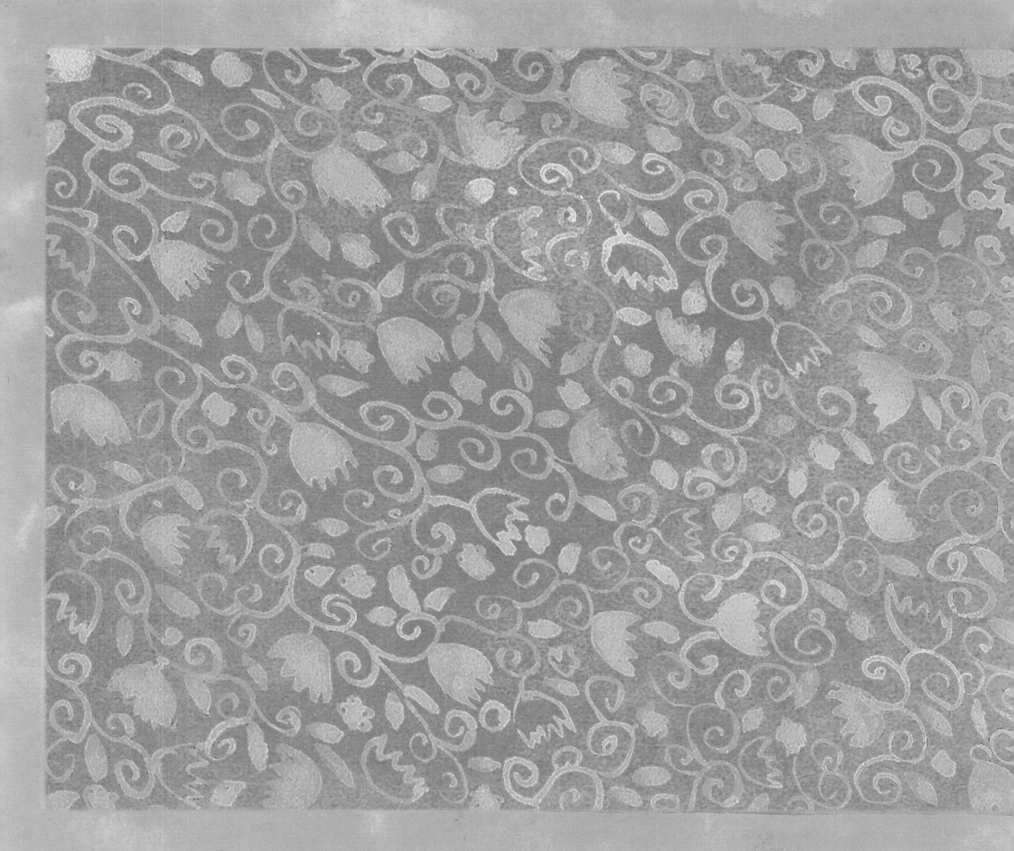